For Orson Ward
and his parents

i.m. Ted Owen

With thanks to Alice, Frank and Elizabeth, and everyone who helped Up In Arms come home to this stage; Joanna Read, Caroline Leslie and everyone at LAMDA who supported the play's development; Gareth Machin, Sebastian Warrack and everyone at Wiltshire Creative; Phil Gibby and Arts Council South West; Oberon Books; Simon, Fitz and all at Dalzell and Beresford; the company, and Charlie.

T0347881

Federico García Lorca

BLOOD WEDDING

Retold by Barney Norris

OBERON BOOKS
LONDON

WWW.OBERONBOOKS.COM

First published in 2020 by Oberon Books Ltd
521 Caledonian Road, London N7 9RH
Tel: +44 (0) 20 7607 3637 / Fax: +44 (0) 20 7607 3629
e-mail: info@oberonbooks.com
www.oberonbooks.com

A catalogue record for this book is available from the British Library.

PB ISBN: 9781786829801
E ISBN: 9781786829818

10 9 8 7 6 5 4 3 2 1

Characters

GEORGIE, 22

ROB, her fiancée, 18

HELEN, Rob's Mum, 40

LEE, 25, Georgie's ex, an Irish traveller

DANNI, 22, Lee's wife

BRIAN, 70, caretaker at the village hall.

*The action takes place round the back of
a village hall in Edington, Wiltshire.*

Blood Wedding was first presented at Salisbury Playhouse on 11th February 2020, with the following cast:

Reece Evans	ROB
Lily Nichol	GEORGIE
Teresa Banham	HELEN
Jeff Rawle	BRIAN
Eleanor Henderson	DANNI
Emmet Byrne	LEE

Director	Alice Hamilton
Designer	James Perkins
Lighting Designer	Johanna Town
Sound Designer	Harry Blake

A Wiltshire Creative and Up In Arms Production, generously supported by Wiltshire Creative's Commissioning Circle.

Up In Arms supported by Frank and Elizabeth Berman

Supported using public funding by
ARTS COUNCIL ENGLAND

This text went to print during rehearsals and as such may differ from the play as performed.

HELEN, GEORGIE and ROB are standing round the back entrance of a typical low-grade Wiltshire village hall – pebbledash, railings, waterproof paint. There's scaffolding over part of the roof, and a big black bin by the door.

ROB: Me and Trev and Jeb were in this wood. Just hanging out. We used to have this sort of den with a mattress where we'd make fires, in the wood where the raves were, and no one ever came by cos it was really far in, and we'd build dens and fuck about and whatever. Tried to make a tiger trap but the sides kept falling in. And we were there one night, right, having a bit of a drink and whatever. We were a bit gone like. And we saw the absolute scariest thing you ever imagined. It was a full moon night, yeah, and we'd had a fire but it'd gone out, cos we were all over the place. I mean I had my kit off like usual, few pints and I've always got my shirt off haven't I. And there were clouds coming over the moon, so it'd be dark and then light. We were messing about boxing or wrestling or something, in the dark, and suddenly the clouds cleared and there was this girl standing by the mattress. Little girl like a kid. I swear we all saw her. Screamed to fuck, didn't we. Then the clouds went over the moon again and she wasn't there any more. Yeah. That's why I believe in ghosts, see.

GEORGIE: You were stoned.

ROB: Yeah, maybe, but all three of us saw her.

HELEN: Rob.

ROB: Sorry.

HELEN: Just remember what it does to people, will you?

ROB: Yeah, all right.

GEORGIE: I used to go to raves in there. Think I know where you mean.

ROB: Yeah?

GEORGIE: Before your time.

ROB: Probably.

GEORGIE: Definitely. Had some great nights in there. It is quite haunty.

ROB: It is, innit.

HELEN: It's just the shadows, they play tricks with people's eyes.

GEORGIE: Yeah, probably. And the weed and the speed as well.

ROB: Legend!

HELEN: You two.

GEORGIE: Sorry.

HELEN focuses her anger on the bin by the back of the hall.

HELEN: They'll probably move that when we get round to show time.

ROB: This isn't even the entrance, Mum.

HELEN: No, but –

ROB: This is the back door, no one would see this, so why would they move it? They have to have a bin somewhere, don't they.

HELEN: Probably get it out of sight when there's guests.

GEORGIE: There's a notice board though, look, Rob.

HELEN: Yeah.

ROB: What does that mean?

GEORGIE: Well, notice board.

ROB: Yeah?

GEORGIE: Means people must come in and out of here, doesn't it.

ROB: Why?

GEORGIE: Well, you'd put it where people would see, a notice board. Put it where people would notice.

ROB: You might not.

HELEN: The thing about those big wooden ones, they don't look like they're opened very often. Haven't even got a proper lock, have they, so I can't believe they're the main entrance.

ROB: He'd open them from the inside, wouldn't he.

HELEN: But how does he get in there to do that in the first place? He must come in through another way. Which is why I'm thinking this must be the door, and that bin must want moving once there's guests.

ROB: This won't be the main door for guests.

GEORGIE tries to get away from the bickering, and forces herself to take an interest in the notice board.

GEORGIE: I like these notice boards, they're interesting, aren't they. People and their funny little lives and what they care about and stuff.

HELEN: Don't get stressed, Rob.

ROB: I'm not.

HELEN: Good. If you were thinking about getting stressed, you needn't.

ROB: The only way of guaranteeing that someone gets stressed out is telling them not to.

HELEN: That's not everyone, lots of people benefit from guidance. You just don't like to be criticised, never have done. That's your rejection complex does that.

ROB: What?

HELEN: You can't take criticism, makes you think you're worthless. I've seen it. I've seen you start physically shaking in HSBC when someone asks you if you want any help.

ROB: No you haven't.

HELEN: I did, I was in town doing the shopping and I saw you through the window by the paying in machine having some kind of trouble. This man standing next to you trying to help. Must have had one of those cheques that wouldn't go in cos it was too folded over. And you were bright red and your hands were shaking and I thought, this poor man talking to you, you're not gonna be nice to him. I didn't go in, I knew you wouldn't want me there. That was the whole point you see, you can't accept help.

ROB: Mum, this never happened.

HELEN: It's my fault really. I used to let you cry sometimes in the cot when I was knackered, leave you to it. They said it was OK in a parenting manual but I knew it felt dodgy. And what a harvest I've reaped, I've reaped the whirlwind.

ROB: Mum.

HELEN: My fault really.

ROB: Where did you even read this?

GEORGIE: What's his name again, this bloke we're meeting?

ROB: Do you think we should call him?

GEORGIE: It was Brian, wasn't it? That was his name?

ROB: Brian. Yeah.

GEORGIE: This is so funny then. Look at that. Come here.

ROB: Where?

GEORGIE: 'Line dancing. Brian your own drinks.' He's written his own name, look.

ROB: Oh my God.

GEORGIE: Look at that!

ROB: That is fucking funny. Mum.

HELEN: Oh, poor man.

GEORGIE: We probably should call him.

HELEN: Ten late now isn't he.

GEORGIE: You got the number babe?

ROB: Yeah, sure, yeah.

HELEN: I mean, if it's worth looking round it at all, of course.

ROB: What?

HELEN: If it's worth having a look at all.

ROB: Why wouldn't it be?

HELEN: Well, I'm just thinking. He's late, so he can't be trusted. The place is a building site.

ROB: It's not a building site.

HELEN: Rubbish everywhere, isn't there, though. It might not be worth going to the trouble if he's not nearby, that's all I'm thinking.

GEORGIE: The thing is Helen, this is the only other place within thirty mile of the church that isn't booked apart from that one that wants three grand.

HELEN: Yeah.

GEORGIE: And we haven't got three grand, have we.

HELEN: No.

GEORGIE: So we sort of do have to look round it, cos there aren't any other options, are there.

HELEN: Maybe, yeah.

ROB: Why maybe?

HELEN: Well –

ROB: What other option is there? We can't change church, we've paid the deposit. And Georgie wants to get married in the church she was baptised in, doesn't she, and that's how you're supposed to do it, that's the traditional thing. So what else are you suggesting?

HELEN: Well you could ask to have the deposit carried forward and see what was available a little further down the line, maybe.

ROB: Mum.

HELEN: Because it might just be that doing it all this quickly isn't actually possible, that's all that's in my mind. There might be a reason people plan these things a bit further in advance than we are at the moment. That's all I'm saying.

ROB: So you think we're getting married too quickly.

HELEN: Well.

ROB: Is that why you're being all mopey?

HELEN: I'm not being mopey!

ROB: To be fair, you've been mopey this whole time.

HELEN: I think that's really unfair.

ROB: It's true, Mum, it can't be unfair if it's true. Unless it's like – leukemia or something.

HELEN: Well if I'm putting such a downer on everything I don't have to be here, I could leave you alone.

GEORGIE: No, Helen.

HELEN: I wouldn't want to make this an unhappy process for you. I don't want that. I'm sorry if that's what's happening. I thought I was doing this to help, but if that's not what I'm doing –

GEORGIE: You are helping, Helen.

HELEN: Maybe it's best if I get out of your hair.

GEORGIE: Come on.

HELEN: No, no. I see it now. I've been silly. I didn't think. Of course you want to do this on your own, this is your thing isn't it, it's your wedding. It's nothing to do with me.

ROB: Well you can't leave now, Mum, we need a lift back to Trowbridge.

HELEN: Well.

GEORGIE: We don't think that, Helen. We don't think you're annoying.

HELEN: I didn't say I was annoying, I said I was under your feet.

7

GEORGIE: We don't think that either.

HELEN: Well I don't want to be where I'm not welcome. I just want to help you be happy, my darling, that's all that I want.

ROB: Mum.

HELEN: I could wait in the car if that helped?

ROB: Don't wait in the car. All I'm saying is that we do need to look round this place.

HELEN: Unless it would be better to hold off and do the wedding a little bit further down the line when it's possible to actually plan for it.

ROB: We want a summer wedding.

HELEN: It's summer every year, Rob.

ROB: Mum, come on.

GEORGIE starts crying.

HELEN: Oh, Georgie, don't get upset.

ROB: Thanks, Mum. Nice one.

The door opens. Enter BRIAN.

BRIAN: Sorry, should I go back in?

GEORGIE: Oh. No, don't go back in, we were –

BRIAN: Having a moment?

BRIAN comes out. The door closes unobtrusively behind him. He doesn't notice.

HELEN: We thought you weren't coming.

BRIAN: Oh, there's no need to get upset on my account love! I been inside, you should have knocked.

HELEN: We did.

BRIAN: Did you? Oh, sorry.

ROB: Do you live in there then?

BRIAN: Sorry?

HELEN: We were just trying to work out which door to meet you at. The big one or this one. Which door you come in through when you – but if you live in there then you wouldn't come in through either door, would you.

BRIAN: I don't live in the hall.

HELEN: Oh.

BRIAN: I'm next door. There's a connecting door to my place in the hall kitchen. I live in the little place attached to the side of this, on the other side, did you see it? I'm Brian.

ROB: Yeah. Sorry, yeah, Rob.

BRIAN: Hello Rob. Well that's the men, how very old fashioned.

GEORGIE: Sorry, I'm Georgie.

BRIAN: OK.

ROB: And this is Helen, my mum.

HELEN: Hi.

BRIAN: So you're having your reception here?

ROB: Well, that's why we want to look round it, yeah. To think about it.

BRIAN: Good. Lot of people do come here for that. We're all set up for that, so no worries.

HELEN: And you're very cheap as well.

BRIAN: Oh well that's Edington see, no one round here's got all that much money.

HELEN: Right.

BRIAN: So we can't charge much, even if it was really nice in there. You have to go where the market takes you, don't you. The world needs one star hotels.

ROB: Sure.

BRIAN: I don't mean us though! Don't worry. We're very nice once you've stuck up a bit of bunting.

HELEN: Isn't everywhere nicer with bunting?

BRIAN: Yeah, I suppose it is, yeah. I don't know why more people don't have it in their day to day lives.

GEORGIE: So you wouldn't be living in there on the day then? If we had our reception here, you wouldn't be like, in the kitchen? Round the food?

BRIAN: No, I'd be home. Unless sometimes the hirer invites me to dinner, otherwise I'll be home. Actually I might not even be there in the evening, I make myself scarce if I can once the music starts. And depending on the sort of bridesmaid you're thinking of having they sometimes go up against my back wall for a bit of you know what with whoever they've bumped into, and no one wants to listen to that. Not without a decent view. So I often go down the Three Daggers for the evening.

ROB: Is that the pub?

BRIAN: That's it, yeah. Swanky now. But I put up with it. If it sells drink it sells drink, you know, a pint's a pint for all that. There's a small group of us old boys in the village who've been widowed, who like to get together for a few drinks of a weekend. Talk about other times.

10

GEORGIE: I'm sorry your wife died.

BRIAN: Thank you, young lady. Twelve year back now. This is her, look.

BRIAN shows them a framed picture of Cath next to the message board.

BRIAN: That's my Cath. She's buried over in Imber with our girl, and I'll join them when the time's right. She used to love this place.

HELEN: Yeah?

BRIAN: We looked after it together. I used to do other jobs as well, but the village gave us the job of looking after it and let us live in the little house. Now they're gonna let me stay on here till I pop my clogs I think, what with everything that happened. I hope they do. I mean they can't ask me to go now I've put the picture up, can they! Our place.

HELEN: That must be nice to feel close to her.

BRIAN: Well, Imber's a fair few mile that way of course. You know about Imber don't you?

GEORGIE: No, sorry.

BRIAN: You don't know Imber?! You must! Famous place! Do you really not know it?

HELEN: It was a village requisitioned by the army in the war. They kicked everybody out.

BRIAN: Kicked my mum and dad out, and me and all, when I was little. And we've never been let back ever since except one day out of each year to walk round the ruins. Used it for firing practice. But us who come from there can be buried in the churchyard. My wife's not from there herself, but we'll be buried together, and that's where I'll be. Means I only get to see her every now and then, which could be better, but that's the way it is, see, that's how we do it. And she's with our girl so they're not on their own. But you're not here to talk about that, we're here to sort out your reception. I promise you'll love it. We're always making improvements. We've got some work on even now look, see that, got a lad going over the roof for me.

HELEN: We wanted to ask you about that, actually.

BRIAN: Oh right?

HELEN: We were just wondering how long you'll be doing whatever you're doing up there, really. Whether that would be up on the day.

BRIAN: Oh, I shouldn't expect so.

HELEN: OK.

BRIAN: He's just patching a bit of leaky roof, I shouldn't think he'll be too long. When are you wanting this for?

ROB: Three weeks tomorrow.

BRIAN: Oh God, that's a bit tight innit? You two on a deadline? Twelve week scan coming up is it?

GEORGIE: We just wanted a summer wedding.

BRIAN: Oh right. Fair enough.

ROB: And we had to go with when the church was free, you know.

HELEN: And they haven't been very organised or proactive about putting everything together.

ROB: All right.

BRIAN: Young love, eh? Well I reckon the scaffold'll probably be down be then.

HELEN: That's good news.

BRIAN: Only a little job as far as I've heard.

ROB: Great.

HELEN: Now that's sorted maybe we should start the tour, what do you think?

BRIAN: Oh yeah, good thought. Hang on though.

ROB: What?

BRIAN: Shut meself out.

HELEN: Oh.

BRIAN: Didn't mean to let it shut behind me. I thought I'd made a mental note. Now I haven't brought my keys.

GEORGIE: Right.

HELEN: So what do we do then?

BRIAN: Oh, no worries. It's just annoying but it's all right. I'll go in through my place then through the kitchen, and back round to here to open it from the inside. All right?

ROB: OK.

BRIAN: Be one minute then. Sorry about this. I'd lead you through that way as well but I like to keep my house my own space, I'm a very private man you see. Sorry. Only meant to open the door and let you in and then you got all upset, didn't you.

GEORGIE: Sorry.

BRIAN: No, forget about it. Hang on.

They watch as he trudges off.

ROB: Brian your own drink.

HELEN: Don't be unkind, Rob.

ROB: Sorry.

GEORGIE: Funny man though.

ROB: Funny.

HELEN: Yeah. Georgie, I didn't mean to upset you earlier, I'm sorry.

GEORGIE: No, I'm sorry, I was being stupid. I just worry that – no.

HELEN: Go on, say.

GEORGIE: Just sometimes I think that you don't like me. I don't fit in.

HELEN: Of course you do. Of course I do.

GEORGIE: You just think we're going too fast?

HELEN: I don't know, love. It's just hard to find everything we need at this notice, isn't it. I think that's stressing me out.

ROB: This looks all right though.

HELEN: Well, we haven't been in yet.

ROB: But he seems all right. I reckon we've found it.

HELEN: If that man is all right, what would count as unacceptable?

ROB: Mum. Come on, this is the place!

HELEN: Yeah, maybe.

GEORGIE: Do you really think so?

ROB: I reckon, yeah. I reckon it works really well.

GEORGIE: I think so too.

ROB: Close enough to the church.

HELEN: Only a twenty mile drive.

ROB: That's close enough. And it's big.

HELEN: Absolutely. Well I can't wait to look around it then, if we're so set on it.

GEORGIE: I know I'm not pulling my weight with the money. Is that what it is?

HELEN: No, Georgie.

GEORGIE: If I had any money I'd put it in, I swear. Or if my Mum was talking to me then I'd ask her, but she's not. I'm really sorry.

HELEN: You don't have to apologise for that, come on.

ROB: I'm covering most of it anyway, aren't I.

HELEN: Absolutely, yeah.

ROB: And my money's your money, innit. That's marriage. Once we're married, my money's your money, so you'll have paid for the wedding.

GEORGIE: Yeah?

ROB: Absolutely, yeah. That's how it works, that's the whole thing.

HELEN: Quite a long way round to his house then back through the hall again, isn't it.

ROB: Unless he's had a heart attack and he's lying in there dead.

GEORGIE: Rob.

ROB: Well he might have done.

HELEN: Probably not though.

ROB: How long would we wait before we broke in and saved him?

The door opens and BRIAN is there.

BRIAN: Here we are then.

HELEN: Oh, lovely.

ROB: We were worried you might have got lost.

BRIAN: What?

ROB: We thought it was a long time. You might have got lost.

HELEN: Rob.

BRIAN: Oh, yeah. I wasn't lost.

ROB: Right.

BRIAN: Come on in and take a look around.

HELEN: You two first.

GEORGIE: Thanks.

HELEN: Do you want me to come in with you?

ROB: Mum.

HELEN: OK, just saying.

They go in. The stage is empty for a moment, then DANNI comes on, pushing a pram, talking on her phone. DANNI is pregnant.

DANNI: I know, yeah. He didn't say anything. I don't know what he said to him. Well he couldn't get home. Yeah he had to walk it. I know, yeah. Course not. No one hitch hikes any more. Well you shouldn't.

GEORGIE comes back out, speaking on her phone.

GEORGIE: No, Mum, it's not the best time right now.

DANNI: Oh my God.

GEORGIE: I'm looking round my / wedding venue aren't I.

DANNI: Just seen someone.

GEORGIE: Well if you ever called I'd have asked you.

DANNI: I might need to go actually.

GEORGIE: I know you are now, but now's a bad time.

DANNI: OK.

DANNI rings off.

GEORGIE: Edington. Near Westbury innit. Yeah, well that's what you're supposed to do, innit, that's the tradition. No it's not wherever the mother lives, it's the church you got baptised in. Look it up.

DANNI: Hiya.

GEORGIE: Sorry? Oh my God.

DANNI: I know.

GEORGIE: No not you.

DANNI: Sorry.

GEORGIE: No I just bumped into someone. Listen I need to go. Yeah. I'm sorry. If you do wanna talk then that's great. You can call me later, OK? And we can talk. No, Mum, I need to go. All right, tomorrow, whatever. Love you.

GEORGIE rings off.

GEORGIE: Hiya Danni.

DANNI: Hello George, come here.

They hug, awkwardly.

GEORGIE: You don't live out here do you?

DANNI: Yeah, I do, yeah.

GEORGIE: I didn't know you lived out here.

DANNI: Moved this way, yeah.

GEORGIE: Fuckin' hell. Isn't that amazing. Amazing. And who's this?

DANNI: Oh this is Kenzie. Just out for his walk.

GEORGIE: Hello baby. Hello darling.

DANNI: Yeah.

GEORGIE: He's lovely.

DANNI: Isn't he, yeah. Have a little sister soon an' all.

GEORGIE: Oh my God really?

DANNI: Yeah, yeah.

GEORGIE: Oh Dan congratulations, that's amazing. You must be so happy.

DANNI: Yeah, we are, yeah.

GEORGIE: Great. Wow. Do you know what you'll call her yet?

DANNI: Not yet no. We thought we'd sort of wait and see.

GEORGIE: Oh lovely.

DANNI: I mean we found out the gender and we know she's fine and all, we just thought wait and see about the name. Cos that's what we did with Kenzie, and when we met him, we just knew. And it was just perfect. You know?

GEORGIE: Yeah, yeah. And are you and Lee still –

DANNI: That's it, yeah.

GEORGIE: Amazing. Sorry, I felt really awkward asking that but it's not awkward, is it.

DANNI: Oh my God no. Of course not, no, not if you don't think so.

GEORGIE: Me? I don't think so.

DANNI: Well then.

GEORGIE: He's got your eyes hasn't he.

DANNI: Yeah? His eyes are closed.

GEORGIE: I mean around the eyes.

DANNI: Oh yeah.

GEORGIE: Lovely. So you're living round these ends?

DANNI: That's it, yeah.

GEORGIE: Bloody hell. Small world.

DANNI: Oh God it is innit?

GEORGIE: Never have expected to find you round here.

DANNI: Oh right.

GEORGIE: What?

DANNI: Oh no, it's just I didn't mean it like that. Small world. I just meant neither of us have got very far, have we.

GEORGIE: Oh right.

DANNI: Cos Durrington's only down the road really, innit.

GEORGIE: Well yeah, I spose so.

DANNI: So small world, you know?

GEORGIE: Yeah I spose so. So you're living round here with Lee?

DANNI: That's it. On the site over the hill. It's nice.

GEORGIE: Great.

DANNI: We've got Sky.

GEORGIE: Well that's good.

DANNI: Yeah, it is, yeah. And did I hear you say you were looking at this place for your wedding reception?

Enter ROB.

ROB: All right George?

GEORGIE: Oh, I'm sorry babe, I just bumped into Danni. D'you remember Danni from school?

ROB: Oh yeah. All right?

DANNI: Hiya.

GEORGIE: Rob was a few years below us in school Dan, d'you remember?

DANNI: Oh right. God, sorry, I didn't recognise you! Long time ago now innit.

ROB: Yeah. I guess so, yeah. I mean for you two anyway. Just last year for me.

DANNI: Oh so you really were quite a few years below, weren't you. That'll be why I don't remember you.

GEORGIE: Four years isn't a big gap really.

DANNI: No, no, sorry. Just in school.

GEORGIE: Yeah, school. But not now.

ROB: Anyway we were just wondering if you were coming back in?

GEORGIE: Yeah, course, yeah. Sorry. We're just looking round.

DANNI: How is it in there?

GEORGIE: Yeah, looks amazing. Really amazing.

DANNI: Good. Cos Lee's been doing the roof, so I know there'd been a leak last winter.

GEORGIE: That's Lee's done that.

DANNI: Yeah. That's actually why I came down here, to bring him his lunch.

GEORGIE: Lee's Danni's partner, I knew him when I was at school, but I haven't seen him in years now have I Dan, haven't seen either of you, have I.

DANNI: No.

ROB: Oh right.

GEORGIE: And this is their baby Kenzie.

ROB: Oh, sorry, I didn't – *(He looks at the baby.)* Yeah, nice.

DANNI: I guess he's not here now then.

GEORGIE: I haven't seen him, no.

DANNI: Brian in?

ROB: He's about.

DANNI: Well maybe I could just leave these with him then and leave you to it maybe?

GEORGIE: Ok, sure, yeah.

DANNI: Could you watch him just a second, while I pop in? He won't wake up. I'll just give these to Brian.

GEORGIE: OK.

DANNI: One sec.

DANNI exits inside.

ROB: Are you OK?

GEORGIE: Babe I think maybe we should go somewhere else.

ROB: What d'you mean?

GEORGIE: I don't think we should be having the reception round here. I think we should go somewhere else.

ROB: Why? What's happened?

GEORGIE: Nothing, nothing's happened.

ROB: Well something has, what's wrong with it?

GEORGIE: I just think we ought to keep looking, that's all.

ROB: But you heard what Mum said. There isn't anywhere else nearby.

GEORGIE: I know.

ROB: You can't be too demanding, George. If it has to be this year and it has to be that church, we have to find somewhere nearby that's available and we can afford and this is it. This is what there is. I know it's not amazing and I'm sorry it's not more, but it's what we can afford, so if we're doing this this summer we have to make compromises.

GEORGIE: I know.

ROB: I can't just stick it all on credit card and get the better place and hope I'll find a way to pay it off, it's not sensible.

GEORGIE: I know.

Enter HELEN.

HELEN: Guys, I really don't have that much more small talk to go through with this man, are we looking round the hall or not?

DANNI re-enters at some point over these lines.

ROB: Well Georgie says she doesn't want to.

HELEN: Ah.

GEORGIE: I'm not saying it's not good enough.

ROB: What are you saying then?

GEORGIE: It's just. I'm just not sure it's the vibe that we're looking for.

ROB: The vibe?

GEORGIE: You know.

HELEN: Well we should go somewhere else then.

ROB: We've literally just done this, we can't afford anywhere else.

GEORGIE: Unless like an outdoor one?

HELEN: Or –

ROB: Mum can you not say postpone it another fucking time.

HELEN: If there isn't a place –

ROB: Shut up, Mum! Why do you have to be like this? Always got a better idea haven't you, always know how it ought to be done, and you don't, you're just saying whatever comes into your head, why should we have to listen to it?

HELEN: I'm just offering –

ROB: This is what Dad didn't know how to put up with.

GEORGIE: Rob.

HELEN: That's what he says to you is it?

ROB: Yes, it fucking is.

HELEN: If he ever bothers to pick up the phone to you.

ROB: We talk a lot, we go for pints.

HELEN: I'm just trying to be a devil's disciple.

ROB: A devil's disciple?

HELEN: Advocate. You know what I mean. Don't be angry with me Rob, I'm trying to help.

ROB: Then stop. It doesn't help.

GEORGIE: I don't think she's exactly –

HELEN: I'm sorry darling. Don't be angry with me, I'm sorry.

ROB: Just fucking infuriating, all right? Just – oh, fuck. I'm sorry I snapped.

HELEN: I didn't mean to butt in.

ROB: All right.

HELEN: It's my abandonment complex, that's all, I just want you to be happy so you won't leave me on my own. So I say too much, I always say too much.

ROB: Mum, stop reading whatever magazine is telling you all this.

HELEN: It's not a magazine, it's your sainted father did this actually.

DANNI: I feel like I should go.

HELEN: Oh, I'm sorry, look, we shouldn't be doing this now. Rob, I'm sorry. Let's put it back in its box, shall we?

ROB: All right. So Georgie, what are you saying you want to do?

GEORGIE: Well –

ROB: It's you says you want to do this this summer. We can't do it outside. If we do it outside it'll rain, swear down.

GEORGIE: All right, let's do this then.

ROB: Yeah?

GEORGIE: Yeah. I'm sorry. I was having a panic.

ROB: Panic over?

GEORGIE: Yeah.

ROB: All right.

GEORGIE: All right.

ROB: Safe.

DANNI: That's lovely.

GEORGIE: Exciting.

ROB: Yeah!

Enter BRIAN.

BRIAN: Not much point me showing myself round. Oh, hello Kenzie!

DANNI: He's asleep.

BRIAN: He can't answer me back anyway, dunno why I bother. You know this lot Dan?

25

DANNI: Yeah, I do yeah. Me and Georgie were at school together.

BRIAN: Right.

HELEN: So are we going to go for this?

GEORGIE: Yeah. It's lovely, yeah. Let's do it.

HELEN: All right. We'd like to rent it for that weekend then.

BRIAN: Great. So it's three twenty plus VAT per day.

HELEN: That price is per day?

BRIAN: That's it.

HELEN: You said that was the whole weekend.

ROB: Your website says that's the cost for the whole weekend.

BRIAN: Does it? I don't think it does. I'm afraid it's the price per day.

ROB: It doesn't matter.

HELEN: Rob?

ROB: Come on, let's fucking do it, it doesn't fucking matter. We only have to pay the deposit now anyway, right?

BRIAN: That's right.

ROB: So it doesn't matter. We'll have it.

BRIAN: Lovely. Well if you come with me we can get the forms signed.

ROB: All right.

BRIAN: The deposit's ten per cent, I can take a cheque, and what I do is I don't cash it till the booking's done, cos I know it can help with cashflow to hold off a bit.

HELEN: That's very kind of you.

ROB: Would you be all right to do a cheque then Mum?

HELEN: Yep, absolutely. Shall we go in and get this done?

BRIAN: OK. Kept the door open this time.

ROB: You coming then?

GEORGIE: Gimme a sec. I'll just say goodbye to Dan.

ROB: All right.

HELEN: Come on, Rob, it's your wedding, not mine.

ROB: Yeah.

ROB, HELEN, BRIAN exit.

GEORGIE: Well that's a bit weird, isn't it.

DANNI: He doesn't know about Lee does he.

GEORGIE: No, no. Thought I should leave it in the past,
maybe.

DANNI: Move on from everything, yeah.

GEORGIE: That's it. I mean, yeah. We don't have to stay
fallen out. I'm sorry I said the things I did, back then. We
were just kids, weren't we, we were angry.

DANNI: I did jump in your grave a bit though, I do get that.

GEORGIE: Well.

DANNI: But it's hard, isn't it.

GEORGIE: What?

DANNI: Well, he was the man I was meant to be with, wasn't
he. I mean, look at me. He's the father of my children.
I'm happy forever now. And when you meet the one, then

things are gonna get broken if they have to be. Cos that's what it's like. Love doesn't always behave well, does it.

GEORGIE: No.

DANNI: I'm sorry I didn't remember Rob. He would have been year seven when I left though, wouldn't he.

GEORGIE: Yeah.

DANNI: Keep you young.

GEORGIE: Yeah.

DANNI: You're only as old as the man who's feeling you up.

GEORGIE: Right.

DANNI: Has it been quick then, the wedding?

GEORGIE: Yeah. I guess it has been quite quick. We just. We got engaged, Rob proposed, and I think when he proposed he thought it might be a longer-term thing. The actual wedding. But we talked about what we wanted to do and I got this feeling that it was like, exactly what I needed, you know?

DANNI: Right.

GEORGIE: Exactly what I needed to lift me up out of things.

DANNI: Like what?

GEORGIE: It's hard to explain. Life's just been tough for a little while.

DANNI: I'm sorry.

GEORGIE: You know. Things broke down with my mum and I was sofa surfing, and that fucked me up, so I ended up losing my job. I was turning it round, I was getting control.

But then he proposed and I thought – wedding. Wedding could snap me right out of it.

DANNI: Well done mate.

GEORGIE: Thank you.

DANNI: Yeah. Well I'll leave you to it maybe.

GEORGIE: Sure.

DANNI: God knows where Lee's at, if he's not here. Supposed to be working. Well. See you in a few weeks mate.

DANNI exits.

GEORGIE: Yeah.

GEORGIE is alone for a moment. Enter ROB, HELEN and BRIAN.

HELEN: OK love?

GEORGIE: Yeah.

BRIAN: You've hardly seen inside, sure you're happy with it?

GEORGIE: No, it's lovely, don't worry. It's just what we want.

BRIAN: All right.

ROB: We're gonna have a wicked day here.

BRIAN: You sure you're happy, young lady?

GEORGIE: Yeah. Absolutely, yeah.

BRIAN: Well just give us a ring if you want anything. The giving of rings, that's what it's all about, right?

ROB: Yeah.

BRIAN: And I'll see you again in three weeks.

HELEN: Thank you.

BRIAN: I look forward to it. Safe journey.

GEORGIE: Thanks.

Brian goes back in, closing the door behind him.

HELEN: We all OK then?

GEORGIE: I'm really sorry I've been weird.

ROB: It's all right.

GEORGIE: It's just that this is everything. Doing this, it's everything for me.

ROB: Yeah. We're gonna be happy.

HELEN: She a friend of yours then, that girl?

GEORGIE: Yeah, that's it. Old friend, I haven't seen her in ages. She's from Durrington too, but she moved over here with her partner, so.

HELEN: Lovely.

GEORGIE: Yeah. Nice to see her. I do think it's perfect here, I'm sorry I spent so much time talking to her. I think this'll be perfect for us.

ROB: Yeah?

GEORGIE: Absolutely.

ROB: Well then that's all right.

HELEN: Shall we start back into town then? I've got work in an hour.

GEORGIE: Sorry Helen.

HELEN: No no, all fine, just glad we've found somewhere so now we can get on with it.

GEORGIE: Yeah.

ROB: Do you think we should have a theme?

GEORGIE: What?

ROB: Like, do you think we should decorate it like it's a James Bond wedding or something?

GEORGIE: Why?

ROB: I just saw people do it sometimes, thought it was cool.

GEORGIE: Why would the theme be James Bond?

ROB: Well it probably wouldn't be, that was just an example. You'd pick one more in keeping with the location, wouldn't you. Appropriate.

GEORGIE: What would that be?

ROB: Well we could do *Command and Conquer*.

HELEN: Rob.

ROB: Cos it's a bit bunker, innit. *Command and Conquer* wedding, like everyone was in uniform?

GEORGIE: I don't wanna do that.

ROB: All right.

HELEN: I don't think you need a theme.

ROB: Just if we thought of a good one though, maybe we could do it?

GEORGIE: Yeah. If we thought of a good one, maybe.

ROB: And not Marvel, that wouldn't be good, would it?

GEORGIE: I don't think so.

ROB: I didn't think so either. Just thought I'd check. I'll keep thinking.

HELEN: You'll be all right without a theme.

ROB: We'll see. Not like a tango theme or something? If everyone had maracas and we did something like a mock bull fight? Really passionate costumes. Or we could probably get a real bull, thinking about it. Be good, that. Imagine going to a wedding with a real bull.

GEORGIE: We'll keep thinking about it.

ROB: Yeah, totally. Come on then.

HELEN: When you're ready.

They start to exit.

ROB: I'm ready, I was just thinking wasn't I.

HELEN: All right love, come on.

They exit.

2

Dawn is breaking. The scaffolding has gone. LEE enters, carrying a bottle of beer, empties it down his throat, goes to the hall and clambers athletically onto the roof, settling himself above the door. He watches the sun rise. Enter BRIAN, carrying a ladder and a lightbulb.

BRIAN: Lee.

LEE: Brian.

BRIAN: All right?

LEE: All right.

BRIAN: You're on the roof.

LEE: Mm.

BRIAN: Roof's all finished.

LEE: Just – checking it over.

BRIAN: Oh right. I gotta open up.

> *BRIAN puts the ladder against the wall, climbs the ladder, replaces a lightbulb in a light fixture above the door.*

LEE: Oh right.

BRIAN: Got a wedding in the day.

LEE: Why they want in so early?

BRIAN: Money.

LEE: Oh yeah.

BRIAN: Didn't want the extra cost of setting up last night. They want to do it all in one day.

LEE: Right.

BRIAN: So they'll put out the tables all stressed out this morning.

LEE: Money.

BRIAN: Yeah. If I let one booking off I'd end up hearing from all of them.

LEE: Yeah.

BRIAN: I do feel sorry for them, but I can only do what I can do, you know?

LEE: Yeah.

BRIAN: That's the way it is for all of us.

LEE: Yeah.

BRIAN: Look all right up there then?

LEE: Oh yeah.

BRIAN: You been drinking, Lee?

LEE: What?

BRIAN: Have you been to bed yet mate? You look a bit wasted.

LEE: I'm all right.

BRIAN has finished. He climbs back down.

BRIAN: 'Trouble at mill'?

LEE: Something like that.

BRIAN: How's Danni?

LEE: All right.

BRIAN: And the little one.

LEE: All right.

BRIAN: All right. How's money?

LEE: I'm fine, Brian, don't worry about me.

BRIAN: All right. There's always odd jobs to be found, Lee, if you need them. That's all I'm saying. You just ask, all right?

LEE: All right.

BRIAN: Watching the sun rise.

LEE: Yeah.

BRIAN: Peaceful.

LEE: It would be.

BRIAN: All right. Bit overcast.

LEE: Yeah.

BRIAN: They'll be here before long though.

LEE: OK.

BRIAN: You won't stay up there all day, will you.

LEE: No.

BRIAN: All right.

LEE: I was hoping the sky'd be clearer than this is.

BRIAN: Yeah?

LEE: I just missed the sunset last night. Wanted to see the sun rising.

BRIAN: Yeah.

LEE: I was walking home and I noticed the late light on the fields. And I was right by the path up onto the hill, so I thought, let's see the land catch fire, you know? You know, when it's just meeting the horizon. When the light's horizontal. And you get just a minute of every field lit up like flames.

BRIAN: Oh yeah.

LEE: So I tried to leg it up the path, get as far as the edge bench, you know? But I was too late. It happened when I was halfway up, and still in the gulley. I got a glimpse and not the whole thing. So I was hoping for a show this morning to make up for it.

BRIAN: No luck.

LEE: I went on up to the top anyway. Watched it get dark. And the lights were coming on in all the houses, I could see Melksham and Devizes and the lights on the A361, all orange. I could see the cars going places. I thought of Chippenham out there in the distance, and the M4. I've been doing a job over Chippenham.

BRIAN: Oh yeah?

LEE: Old house. Sixties or something. All wants tearing out and doing again.

BRIAN: Right.

LEE: Then it got dark and I still didn't wanna go home. So I went and bought some bottles and I stayed out, then I stayed at a mate's. And I was just walking past just now and I thought, I'm still not ready. I still don't wanna go home.

BRIAN: You wanna come down and have a cuppa?

LEE: No, you're all right. I'll fuck off in a minute, I promise.

BRIAN: OK.

LEE: I will, I'm sorry. I just thought there might be a show.

BRIAN: I'd better go in and get the lights on before anyone gets here, really.

LEE: OK.

BRIAN: Take your time, yeah? They won't see you here with any luck. They'll probably come round the front.

LEE: All right.

BRIAN opens the door and goes in, leaving it open behind him. Enter HELEN, laden with bags and boxes.

HELEN: Hello.

LEE: Oh. All right.

HELEN: I thought the roof was going to be done?

LEE: Oh, yeah, it is, yeah. Brian just asked me to give it a last once over.

HELEN: OK. Is he here?

LEE: He's just gone in.

HELEN: Right. Cos I'm hoping to load in through the big front doors, if he can unlock those.

LEE: Yeah. He's just gone to do it. Thought you'd come that way.

HELEN: This bin will stay here then, will it?

LEE: For the caterers.

HELEN: I suppose it's the back door.

LEE: You having caterers?

HELEN: Yes, of course.

LEE: Cool. They'll need it.

HELEN: Well I'd better go in.

LEE: All right.

HELEN: Sorry, do I know you? You seem familiar to me.

LEE: Oh, right.

HELEN: Did you used to live in Durrington?

LEE: Yeah.

HELEN: I remember you. You used to hang around the school gates.

LEE: I had a couple of girlfriends went to that school.

HELEN: You didn't go there.

LEE: Nah. I didn't do a whole lot of school.

HELEN: Did you not?

LEE: I'm a traveller, aren't I. Hard going to school when you move around.

HELEN: Of course.

LEE: That's the way my Dad made his money, see. And how I do it too.

HELEN: You travel around.

LEE: Got a base here now though. Base in Edington.

HELEN: Right. Hope it looks all right up there.

LEE: What?

HELEN: The roof.

LEE: Oh, yeah. Yeah, it's fine.

HELEN: Bye then.

LEE: Bye.

HELEN exits into the hall. A moment passes. Enter BRIAN.

BRIAN: All right Lee?

LEE: Yeah.

BRIAN: All looking all right up there then?

LEE: You know it is.

BRIAN: All right.

LEE: She asked you to get me off the roof has she?

BRIAN: Something like that.

LEE: Yeah, thought she might.

BRIAN: Only cos it makes her anxious. And I'm already in trouble cos I can't find the front door key.

LEE: I'm not gonna nick the cake or nothing.

BRIAN: She doesn't think you're gonna nick anything.

LEE: I think it crossed her mind.

BRIAN: Don't be bloody touchy. It just makes her think maybe the roof's not finished and I don't want her thinking that or next thing she'll start off asking for discounts.

LEE: All right.

BRIAN: She doesn't think you're here to nick anything.

LEE: I've never gone on the rob, you know. Never in all my life.

BRIAN: I know it.

LEE: Not worth it, is it. Not if you can work.

BRIAN: If you can.

LEE: And I always have.

BRIAN: Yup.

LEE: Never went on the rob.

BRIAN: All right, good for you. You'll come down then will you?

LEE: Yeah, all right.

BRIAN: Sorry. Only cos she asked.

LEE: It's all right.

BRIAN: I'll see you then.

LEE: Sure.

BRIAN goes back in. LEE lowers himself down from the roof, and stands in front of the door. GEORGIE enters and stops when she sees him.

LEE: Fancy seeing you here.

GEORGIE: Fuck's sake.

What are you doing here?

LEE: Good to see you too.

GEORGIE: I can't talk to you now.

LEE: Yeah?

GEORGIE: Lee.

LEE: I didn't know whether you'd be here this morning.

GEORGIE: Hung around like a bad smell just in case.

LEE: Something like that, yeah.

GEORGIE: I don't want to talk to you today.

LEE: What you got there?

GEORGIE: Honeymoon bag.

LEE: What?

GEORGIE: It doesn't matter.

LEE: What is it?

GEORGIE: We're going on honeymoon straight from here, so I need to leave my bag here for when the car comes.

LEE: Where you going?

GEORGIE: I don't want to talk about it with you.

LEE: Yeah, but where are you going?

GEORGIE: Benahavis.

LEE: Where's that?

GEORGIE: It's in Spain. We're flying from Bristol airport in the morning.

LEE: Nice.

GEORGIE: It is nice, yeah.

LEE: I'm not being sarcastic, G. It sounds really nice.

GEORGIE: I can't talk to you today.

LEE: No one'll see us, chill out. They're all round the front setting up your tables.

GEORGIE: It's not just about other people.

LEE: What?

GEORGIE: I don't want talk to you cos I don't wanna talk to you. It's not about what other people think. I'm getting married today.

LEE: Danni was a bit fucked up seeing you here, you know.

GEORGIE: Why?

LEE: She thinks I've still got a thing for you.

GEORGIE: Have you?

LEE: For a girl who dumped me because of who my parents are?

GEORGIE: Lee.

LEE: That's what happened, innit. I was the wrong race, innit.

GEORGIE: I had to get away from you.

LEE: Yeah but why was that?

GEORGIE: You know my relationship with my dad was really bad, he was really controlling –

LEE: There are some things that ought to snap you out of that shit. Some things you should hear and think, nah, that is the bad guy. You went along with it.

GEORGIE: I wasn't good at standing up for myself.

LEE: They told you you had to choose between me and them, and you chose. Cos your mum and dad told you they didn't like boys like me. My type, yeah? Fuck yeah. The last prejudice no one anywhere gives any fucks about.

GEORGIE: It wasn't good us being together, I was better away from you, I was.

LEE: Were you? Well that's all right then. You met my boy.

GEORGIE: Yeah.

LEE: He's beautiful. He's brilliant.

GEORGIE: Yeah.

LEE: Love him.

GEORGIE: Good.

LEE: How did it make you feel?

GEORGIE: What?

LEE: Seeing him.

GEORGIE: I dunno. He was lovely.

LEE: Yeah?

GEORGIE: I thought he was sweet, yeah.

LEE: Right.

GEORGIE: What, do you want me to say I was jealous?

LEE: Were you?

GEORGIE: We're done, Lee. I'm getting married.

LEE: D'you think you'll go through with it then?

GEORGIE: What?

LEE: I mean, can you do it? And say the words.

GEORGIE: You did.

LEE: Yeah.

GEORGIE: Can't be that hard then.

LEE: We'll see.

GEORGIE: I'll go through with it, yeah.

LEE: And will you be thinking of him when you say it? Or will you be thinking of me?

GEORGIE: Fuck off.

LEE: I'm just asking.

GEORGIE: We're done.

LEE: You're fake news.

GEORGIE: Fuck off.

LEE: You are, I can see it in your face. You're fake news. Who is he anyway?

GEORGIE: I knew him from school.

LEE: Bit younger, Danni said.

GEORGIE: Yeah.

LEE: Bit of a cradle snatcher sort of situation.

GEORGIE: I don't have to listen to this.

LEE: It's very quick, innit. Field to fork.

GEORGIE: What do you know about it?

LEE: You were still single on Facebook in April.

GEORGIE: How d'you know that?

LEE: I still have a look. I'm not too proud to say. I still check. You like that, don't you. That makes you feel good.

GEORGIE: It doesn't make me feel anything, it makes me feel bored.

LEE: You like it.

GEORGIE: He asked and I said yes, it's always quick, that's how long it takes.

LEE: I asked.

GEORGIE: My life is different now.

LEE: I heard you'd been in trouble. That's what you told Dan.

GEORGIE: Things went wrong.

LEE: You think he's a lifebelt.

GEORGIE: What do you mean?

LEE: You think he might stop you from drowning.

GEORGIE: I'm gonna get my life back on track thanks to him, if that's what you mean. Because of today, because of this.

LEE: Can't you be honest with me?

GEORGIE: I'm telling you what I feel.

LEE: All right.

GEORGIE: I have to go.

LEE: Will you do something for me?

GEORGIE: What?

LEE: Will you be honest with yourself?

GEORGIE: What d'you mean?

LEE: When you're standing there, and you're looking at him, if you find it's not him that you're thinking about, don't just ignore it.

GEORGIE: I won't have to.

LEE: No?

GEORGIE: I'm marrying someone I love.

LEE: I hope so. Life is too long not to, I tell you. Life's too long to just make the best of things. What will you do?

GEORGIE: What do you mean?

LEE: If you get there and find that you're thinking of me, then what will you do about it? Will you still say the words? I think you're braver than that.

Enter DANNI.

DANNI: Lee.

LEE: All right Danni.

DANNI: You all right?

LEE: Yeah.

DANNI: Been having fun?

LEE: What?

DANNI: Where did you fucking go last night? Why haven't you been picking up your phone?

GEORGIE: Dan, I have to go in, OK, I'm gonna leave you to it.

DANNI: Lee?

LEE: Just be honest with yourself, yeah, G?

DANNI: What?

LEE: Be honest.

Enter HELEN.

HELEN: Georgie.

GEORGIE: All right Helen?

HELEN: Everything all right?

GEORGIE: It's fine. You remember Danni? My friend from school.

HELEN: Yeah, all right.

GEORGIE: And this is Danni's husband.

HELEN: Yeah, we met.

GEORGIE: I have to drop this off.

GEORGIE marches into the hall past HELEN.

HELEN: You two OK?

DANNI: We're fine. We're just leaving.

HELEN: OK. Good bye then.

LEE: Yeah, bye.

HELEN exits.

DANNI: What the fuck Lee?

LEE: Don't start.

DANNI: I can't believe you stayed out all night and didn't call me.

LEE: Sorry.

DANNI: And what are you doing coming here?

LEE: I was walking past.

DANNI: Haven't you got any pride, though, haven't you got any shame?

LEE: What?

DANNI: Turning up and talking to her now, you know what you look like.

LEE: No.

DANNI: You know what it makes me look like. And Kenzie. Your family.

LEE: It doesn't make anyone look anything, I was walking by, I saw someone I knew, I talked to them.

Enter HELEN, carrying packaging out to the bin.

HELEN: Look, can I just ask you two to explain to me what's going on here?

LEE: Sorry?

HELEN: I'm trying to get on with work inside, I've got a hell of a lot I have to do, and there's this sort of welcome committee getting together round the back door and Georgie is not calm, and I don't really understand what you're doing here.

DANNI: I'm really sorry, we're just about to go.

HELEN: I don't really like having people round the margins like this, it's stressing me out. This is my son's wedding day. My son's getting married. And it's great to meet friends of Georgie, but you're stressing me out and stressing Georgie out, and I don't have time for it. Not today. I'm getting today right for my son, all right?

Enter ROB.

ROB: All right?

HELEN: Rob?

ROB: All right Danni? It's Rob, we met the other week.

DANNI: Yeah, I remember.

HELEN: You're really early.

ROB: Lots to do, innit. You must be Lee.

LEE: All right.

ROB: Good to meet you.

They shake hands.

ROB: You know George a bit?

LEE: Yeah, I do, yeah.

HELEN: Rob I think you might need to drive round the block
again.

ROB: What?

HELEN: Georgie's inside.

ROB: What?

HELEN: She's dropping something off, I don't know what.

LEE: Honeymoon bag.

HELEN: Yeah. I think you need to go away and come back
again, love, you can't see her.

ROB: Fucking hell.

HELEN: We should shut the – oh my God she's actually
coming.

ROB: Shit!

DANNI: Oh my God you can't see her, it's luck!

ROB: I know.

HELEN: Georgie, stop. Just stop there. Rob's here.

GEORGIE: *(Off.)* What?

HELEN: Yeah, he's turned up early.

GEORGIE: *(Off.)* Oh, fucking hell.

ROB: All right George?

GEORGIE: *(Off.)* Rob!

ROB: All right fiancée?

HELEN: Robert, be quiet.

ROB: All right.

LEE: This is fucked.

GEORGIE: *(Off.)* Is that Lee? Are Lee and Danni still there?

DANNI: All right George.

HELEN: Right, look, here's what we're gonna do.

GEORGIE: *(Off.)* OK.

HELEN: Rob, you have to turn round, and Georgie you walk out past him.

ROB: No way. Why can't she just go out the front?

HELEN: He's lost the key.

BRIAN: I've lost the key.

HELEN: Just turn round so she can go past Rob.

GEORGIE: *(Off.)* That'll still be bad luck won't it?

HELEN: No, it's if you see each other.

GEORGIE: *(Off.)* Only if you actually see each other?

HELEN: Well if it isn't then you've already ruined it, haven't you, so let's say it is. All right? Let's just turn around, and Georgie you walk past him, and I reckon if you don't touch each other or turn round or anything, you'll be all right.

GEORGIE: *(Off.)* You up for it Rob?

ROB: Yeah, guess so, all right.

HELEN: Well turn round then.

ROB turns round.

HELEN: All right love.

GEORGIE enters. She sees ROB. She sees LEE there as well.

ROB: All right fiancée?

GEORGIE: Shut up.

HELEN: Don't talk to each other! Go on Georgie, go and get ready all right?

ROB: See you later yeah?

GEORGIE: All right.

LEE: See you later G.

GEORGIE: Love you Rob.

ROB: Love you too babe.

HELEN: Go on, go and get in your car.

GEORGIE: All right. See you later.

GEORGIE exits. ROB turns round.

ROB: Fucking hell.

HELEN: You didn't see her, did you?

ROB: I swear it. I swear I didn't.

HELEN: All right then. That's fine then. That's probably not bad luck.

ROB: Bloody hell. Absolute mad scenes.

HELEN: Yeah.

ROB: Absolute mad 'ead 'ere, nearly jinx my own wedding. What am I like?

LEE: Yeah.

ROB: Such banter.

LEE: Absolutely masses of banter.

ROB: Yeah, he gets it see Mum!

HELEN: I'm sure in time we'll all have a laugh about it.

ROB: She all right though? Georgie, she cool yeah?

HELEN: She's fine, I think.

ROB: What are you two up to anyway, just wishing her luck?

DANNI: Sorry?

ROB: Did you come to wish Georgie luck?

DANNI: Oh. Well.

LEE: That's it, yeah.

ROB: Sweet.

LEE: And you, obviously.

ROB: Thanks. Legend. Tell you what though. This is so rude of us but has anyone actually invited you two to come tonight?

DANNI: Sorry?

ROB: Fuck have we not? Guys you ought to come! I'm so sorry, we should have said before, you fuckin' live here and you're Georgie's mates, you should come along this evening for the party. Right Mum?

HELEN: Is the guest list full though?

ROB: No way, loads of room. What are you doing tonight?

LEE: We're free.

DANNI: I don't think we can come, Lee.

ROB: Oh what you doing?

LEE: Nothing. We're free. We'll come down.

DANNI: Lee.

LEE: Be fun.

ROB: Wicked. Absolute legend mate. Sorry, we should have thought of it. You can come for the ceremony if you like, there's room in the church, but if you just wanna come for the evening, that's the good bit innit, you wanna come for the fucking DJ. Not for the drinks though, I respect that, you don't have to drink if you're pregnant, maximum respect.

DANNI: All right. Do you want to ask Georgie that she's OK with it?

ROB: Can't talk to her can I. But you're her mates, she'll love it. Wedding surprise.

LEE: Legend.

ROB: Yes mate.

HELEN: I could ask Georgie if she's OK with it?

ROB: What's the point? Let's make it a nice surprise.

DANNI: All right.

ROB: If you wanna come to the service that's in Urchfont at two in the church. It's like dress-up but not proper dress-up. I've gone full Moss Bros obviously but you don't have to. And if you just wanna come later on, we'll be here from like fourish I guess, and we'll cut the cake and whatever and speeches, when's all that Mum?

HELEN: About five.

ROB: Yeah, about five. Be good. It's a buffet. Simpler, innit. And drinks, you stick twenty behind the bar at the start of the evening and then just fill your boots. But not if you're not drinking, Danni, I totally respect that.

DANNI: OK. Well we'd better get back to the little one I reckon, Lee?

LEE: Yeah, fine. See you later then you two.

ROB: Sweet. See you later.

DANNI: Come on. Bye.

ROB: Yeah, laters!

LEE and DANNI exit.

HELEN: I don't know whether we need them here tonight my love.

ROB: Don't be stress Mum. It'll be a laugh. Georgie's gonna love it.

3

The same spot, that night. Party music. LEE and DANNI are onstage.

DANNI: No, I wanna talk now.

LEE: About what?

DANNI: About you ignoring me all evening.

LEE: How have I been ignoring you?

DANNI: You've barely fucking talked to me.

LEE: Who else have I talked to?

DANNI: I can't be arsed with this. Fuck this. Absolutely fuck it. You know what I'm talking about.

LEE: I don't.

DANNI: You and her.

LEE: There obviously is no me and her. She's swerved me all night.

DANNI: Why are we still together?

LEE: Don't.

DANNI: There's nothing is there.

LEE: What do you mean?

DANNI: You don't feel anything. You haven't been with me for the past fucking year, I dunno, since Kenzie was born, I dunno what did it.

LEE: That's –

DANNI: You're never here, Lee. Not up there. You're always somewhere else. Maybe you didn't want to be a father.

LEE: Of course I fucking did.

DANNI: You just haven't loved me since Kenzie was born. Or maybe I just never noticed till then, maybe you never felt anything. But you don't feel anything now. There's nothing here. Except that I love you, and this is your child, and that is your child up there in the caravan sleeping.

LEE: I don't know how to answer you because I don't know what's caused this, I don't know where you're coming from.

DANNI: If you don't want to be with us I don't know whether I want you around.

LEE: What?

DANNI: My life. My family. My children.

LEE: My children too.

DANNI: But if all you do is make me feel this lonely –

LEE: For richer for poorer for better for worse, Dan, don't fuck about, we both said it. You can't just say you'll leave me cos you're having a bad evening.

DANNI: It's not a bad fucking evening Lee, I want you to love me and I don't believe it when you tell me you do. I don't believe it, and if you did, you'd have said something by now, you wouldn't let me keep talking. But there you go, see. You're not saying anything. I don't have to stay with you, you know. And live on that site, and take what I'm given. I could go away I could find a job and look after myself.

LEE: I'm not letting my wife work on some fucking till, that's embarrassing.

DANNI: I'll do whatever I want Lee, it's not your decision. I don't have to be a fucking pikey wife, I could be in control of my life if I wanted.

LEE: Is that what you're calling me now, is it?

DANNI: Why can I only get through to you by trying to hurt you? Why can't I get through to you any way else?

LEE: I'm going for a walk.

DANNI: I'm talking to you.

LEE: I don't wanna talk to you when you're like this, I'm going for a walk.

DANNI: I won't bring my children up around you if you're only gonna hurt us. If the only reason you look after us is that you think you have to, that's what you're doing, you're hurting us.

LEE: Fuck off, Dan. What are you asking me?

DANNI: I want you to love me.

LEE: Why would you want anything from me if you think I'm such a prick?

Enter BRIAN.

BRIAN: All right you two?

DANNI: Fuck's sake.

LEE: All right Brian.

BRIAN: Don't let me interrupt you.

LEE: Nah, you're all right, I was just going for a fag.

BRIAN: How's the party in there?

LEE: Yeah. Yeah it's all right, yeah.

BRIAN: Good. You two enjoying yourselves?

LEE: Absolutely, yeah.

DANNI: Laugh a fucking minute.

BRIAN: Ah. Well, this is always where couples come about now for a set-to when we have a wedding. Don't you worry. I've watched people do it for twenty years and most of them are still married twenty years later. Don't you worry. It's a normal thing having a row. Least you're being honest with each other.

LEE: Yeah.

BRIAN: You'll be all right in the morning.

DANNI: Yeah.

BRIAN: Think of the good things. You remember the morning your little one were baptised?

DANNI: Oh, yeah.

BRIAN: I felt so proud to be asked. You remember the light fell on the water in the priory font. Dazzling, weren't it. Just as the vicar started to speak. And little Kenzie good as gold in white cotton, quiet as a mouse.

DANNI: That was a lovely day.

BRIAN: Just hold to things like that. That's what you're looking after. Not only today, you see, it's everything that's gone before, that's what you have between you. It's all right to have a row sometimes because you'll be all right in the morning. When you wake up you'll still have the light on the water in the font.

LEE: Listen I might just go stretch my legs for five minutes Brian, OK?

BRIAN: Oh sure.

DANNI: Lee.

LEE: I'll see you back in the hall, OK?

DANNI: Lee.

LEE: I'll see you back in the hall.

LEE exits.

BRIAN: You OK Danni?

DANNI: I've gotta go back in, Brian, sorry.

BRIAN: OK.

DANNI exits.

BRIAN: Something I said?

There's a broken bin bag on stage, rubbish strewn over the floor. He starts clearing up, and GEORGIE enters. She smokes a cigarette over the following conversation.

GEORGIE: All right.

BRIAN: *(To the tune of the Bridal March.)* Oh, dah, dah, dah dah, dah, dah, dah dah, dah, dah, dah dah, dah, dah dah, dah, dah dah!

GEORGIE: Yeah.

BRIAN: How'd it go then?

GEORGIE: Yeah, good, yeah. Gets hot in there though.

BRIAN: Oh yeah. I'm sorry about this, you shouldn't have to see this. One of these bags has split and no one's fixed it.

GEORGIE: Sorry.

BRIAN: Not your fault, is it.

GEORGIE: No, but the caterers should have – I'd help, but my dress, you know.

BRIAN: No, you mustn't.

GEORGIE: I should have got an evening dress really. People have them now.

BRIAN: What for?

GEORGIE: For changing into.

BRIAN: What for?

GEORGIE: Well, I dunno. Fashion. To relax.

BRIAN: Oh right.

GEORGIE: You been at the pub then?

BRIAN: Just for my dinner, yeah. I'm not a big drinker really.

GEORGIE: No.

BRIAN: It would have been too easy, to end up in drink once I was – once I was alone again. It would have been so obvious. I don't like doing what people expect of me. I don't like that. Sorry, I shouldn't – you get to thinking, leaning on your elbows over your plate. I shouldn't talk about it all with you.

GEORGIE: You're all right. I'm too hot. Just need a minute.

BRIAN: Oh right.

GEORGIE: D'you think about your wife a lot?

BRIAN: Of course. All the time, of course.

GEORGIE: Yeah. Sorry. Can I ask you something?

BRIAN: Go on.

GEORGIE: Did you love her all your life?

BRIAN: Sorry?

GEORGIE: I was just – you never went off her or anything like that?

BRIAN: God no.

GEORGIE: Sorry. I just don't know what it's going to be like.

BRIAN: Well, it'll be everything, really. A bit of everything. It being your life and all.

GEORGIE: Yeah.

BRIAN: Which will include bad times as well as good.

GEORGIE: Yeah, course, yeah.

BRIAN: You're frightened.

GEORGIE: No, no, I'm just pissed probably. I'm probably just pissed. Can I ask you something?

BRIAN: Go on.

GEORGIE: What happened to your daughter?

BRIAN: Oh. Well she died, unfortunately. Car accident, yeah. You know.

GEORGIE: I'm so sorry.

BRIAN: Well, you know. I'll be with her again before ever so long.

GEORGIE: Yeah.

BRIAN has done all he can tidying.

BRIAN: That's a bit better, innit.

GEORGIE: Thank you. Sorry.

BRIAN: Don't worry, you don't have to say sorry, it's my job. I'll be up tomorrow scrubbing the loos and all.

GEORGIE: Right.

BRIAN: I'm not saying the loos will be bad. Sorry. It's just part of good hygiene, isn't it, it's one of the things I do.

GEORGIE: Sure.

BRIAN: We get much worse than you lot. Some traveller weddings they like to throw rice everywhere. I'm not saying I mind that either, it's their culture, I'm not a racist, honest.

GEORGIE: Sure.

BRIAN: I've got friends who are women, I've got friends who are young. I can't say I have friends from the ethnic minorities because being honest, it's north Wiltshire, who has, but what I'm saying is that I'm a tolerant person. I'm a private man myself and I think everyone else deserves the kingdom of their own life also, don't they.

GEORGIE: Yeah.

BRIAN: You see I do get it. People would assume otherwise to look at me, but I do. The generation before me, they wouldn't have approved of chucking rice per se, but the *right* to chuck rice. That's what they fought for. That's why my poor Dad had such a hard time when the Chinese restaurants and the Indian restaurants were arriving. And all those nice Caribbean boys turned up working on the farms off the Windrush. Cos by inclination he was as bigoted as the next man, back when that wasn't such a pejorative term, you know - but he saw Belsen at the liberation. So he ordered his korma with the rest of us because what else can you do, if you've seen Belsen?

GEORGIE: Right.

BRIAN: I know you understand what I'm saying.

GEORGIE: Yeah. Of course.

BRIAN: I think you are scared.

GEORGIE: I dunno.

BRIAN: What is it then?

GEORGIE: I dunno.

BRIAN: Right.

GEORGIE: I don't feel better.

BRIAN: What do you mean?

GEORGIE: I thought that I'd get something back. The reason I first loved Rob, he still remembered me how people used to think I was. When I was still at school, and I felt beautiful, and people thought something good was gonna happen to me. People thought I'd be someone. He still looked at me like I was glowing, like how I used to feel. When really all that stopped when I left school. But he was a lot younger than me at school, he still looked up to me a bit like. In awe of me like. So it was like he saw the old me. I reckoned if I was close to him I'd get the old me back. But I can't feel anything. I just feel the same.

Enter HELEN.

HELEN: All right love?

GEORGIE: Oh, hiya. Just getting some fresh air, I was boiling. Thought I was gonna pass out.

HELEN: Oh yeah. Hi Brian.

BRIAN: All right?

GEORGIE: Brian's clearing up round the bins.

HELEN: Mm. Having a good evening.

When BRIAN has done the clearing he can, he smokes a cigarette at the edge of the stage.

GEORGIE: Oh, wicked, yeah.

HELEN: Good. It's been amazing, hasn't it.

GEORGIE: Yeah.

HELEN: Those two girls are still fighting over your bouquet.

GEORGIE: Neither of them caught it, they dropped it on the floor.

HELEN: Yeah, but little girls like to imagine getting married.

GEORGIE: I know, yeah. Funny innit.

HELEN: Why?

GEORGIE: Well. They could dream of astronauts or anything, couldn't they.

HELEN: But getting married is the happiest thing.

GEORGIE: Yeah.

HELEN: You coming back in?

GEORGIE: In a minute, yeah.

HELEN: I've got some gorgeous snaps of you two cutting the cake.

GEORGIE: Yeah?

HELEN: The smiles on your faces. So lovely.

GEORGIE: Oh, lovely.

HELEN: You feeling all right?

GEORGIE: Fine.

HELEN: Good. I'm a very proud mum today. A very proud mother-in-law.

GEORGIE: Thank you.

HELEN: Dream of this day all your life, don't you. I have. My boy getting married. Ever since he was little I've wondered what it would be like. My last job really.

GEORGIE: How d'you mean?

HELEN: Well, weddings mean different things for different people. For you two, it's the start of something. For me it's the day I finally lose my son. Or give him away, say goodbye to him, I don't know the right phrase really.

GEORGIE: I hope you don't think it's like that.

HELEN: No, but it is a little really. For all mothers, it is like that a bit. You'll know one day maybe. You grieve a little on red letter days for all the times they remind you of that won't come again. His childhood and my youth. But I know that you'll look after him.

GEORGIE: Yeah.

HELEN: I know you'll love him like I do.

GEORGIE: I do, yeah.

HELEN: Well that's all right then. It's been funny having it happen so fast, I've wondered sometimes whether I know you well enough. Whether he knows you well enough. But as long as you love him and both of you do all you can, I think that's enough, isn't it. You two are going to make a beautiful family together. A beautiful life.

GEORGIE: My mum being OK?

HELEN: She's a very vigorous dancer.

GEORGIE: I'll calm her down in a minute. Just once I've cooled down, you know?

HELEN: OK. Well I'd better go back in.

GEORGIE: OK.

HELEN: See you in a minute then.

GEORGIE: OK.

HELEN goes back in.

BRIAN: That was a little bit –

GEORGIE: Oh, I can't talk about it. You know what, I can't do it actually, and I don't even know why I should.

BRIAN: What?

GEORGIE: Everyone saying it's my day, this is my big day, why should I pretend I'm feeling happy if I'm not? Why should I have to? I can be what I want to be can't I?

BRIAN: Well. If that's how you feel.

GEORGIE: I don't know, I don't know. I shouldn't have said that I'm sorry.

BRIAN: You're all right.

GEORGIE: I'm saying stupid things, I'm sorry. I am happy. I shouldn't really talk about this.

BRIAN: OK. Emotional day.

GEORGIE: Yeah.

BRIAN: Maybe I ought to leave you to it.

GEORGIE: All right.

BRIAN: I hope I haven't upset you at all.

GEORGIE: No, I'm fine.

BRIAN: All right. Well congratulations to you.

GEORGIE: Why are they in Imber?

BRIAN: Sorry?

GEORGIE: Your wife and your daughter. Why did you want them so far away?

BRIAN: They're not far from anywhere. That's where my heart is, they're at the centre.

GEORGIE: Did you ever live there?

BRIAN: A couple of years, as a boy. Might be I'm the last living soul who did.

That's the only place we ever thought of as the centre. Cath and I picked that as the place for Emily after she died, and we knew after that that we'd join her when the time came. That's our home. Had to do a lot of arguing to get us all buried there but it had to be done. My life didn't go as well as I'd have liked it, see. We never bought a house. Never had the right salary for that. So I never felt we put down roots, even though we never went anywhere. Now I'm in that cottage out of charity, because I lost my family, because they pity me, the village. I'm a tenant here, shunted here by the council, kept here out of pity. If life had gone different we could have put down roots, done something permanent. But permanence is Imber. That's what we were born to. That's where we belong.

GEORGIE: Right.

BRIAN: The thing is, my dear, that life doesn't go differently. It does what it wants, and most of the time, nearly all the time, what we live is the lives we're born to. And we don't get much say in them. We were born to belong to each other, me and my Cath and my Emily. And we were born to Imber too. So one day we'll all be together there, then no one will be breathing who ever lived there any more, and the myth will be over, and people will visit and see our graves one day a year till they can't read the words on the stones any more. You don't get all that much say in your life, it takes the course it wants.

GEORGIE: Yeah.

BRIAN: That's what I try and tell myself. That's how I find my comfort. If I didn't believe that, I don't know what I'd do. I need to believe we don't get much say in things, or else why did my little girl die? And why did my wife have to die so young? I'll shut up. I'm sorry. I'm gonna go in.

GEORGIE: Sleep well. Sorry about the noise.

BRIAN: Don't you worry about that. Night night.

GEORGIE: Night night.

BRIAN exits. At the edge of the stage, LEE appears, finishing a cigarette. GEORGIE sees him.

GEORGIE: How much of that did you hear then?

LEE: Of your weird evil mother-in-law or Brian talking?

GEORGIE: Quite a lot of it then.

LEE: Yeah, quite a bit, yeah. Sorry. Couldn't help myself.

GEORGIE: Could you not.

LEE: Hey.

GEORGIE: What?

LEE: Your face when you saw I was there.

GEORGIE: Fuck off.

LEE: It was your husband invited us. No gatecrashing.

GEORGIE: I know.

LEE: Thoughtful of him. Your face when you were coming up the aisle.

GEORGIE: Shut up.

LEE: I felt. It was strange seeing you do that. Seeing you walking to the altar and someone else.

GEORGIE: Seriously?

LEE: Why don't you wanna talk to me?

GEORGIE: I just wanna be on my own.

LEE: You told me to go away earlier, we still ended up talking.

GEORGIE: Please fuck off.

LEE: Weird being there.

GEORGIE: You think?

LEE: For you as well?

GEORGIE: Yes, for me as well. You shouldn't have come. Helen told me what had happened. I could have killed Rob.

LEE: Not his fault though, is it.

GEORGIE: Why not?

LEE: If you'd told him the whole story, he wouldn't have done it. Invited us. But obviously you've been holding back.

GEORGIE: I was gonna leave you in the past.

LEE: Were you. I think Danni thinks we're gonna run off together.

GEORGIE: Really?

LEE: I dunno what she thinks. We're not very good at – yeah, we're not very good.

GEORGIE: I'm sorry.

LEE: It'll be all right maybe.

GEORGIE: Yeah.

LEE: I got with her to get at you really. I thought it'd get you back.

GEORGIE: Lee.

LEE: But it didn't work. And then one thing led to another. And now we have kids.

GEORGIE: Yeah, you do.

LEE: You'll have that soon. You'll have all that to discover.

GEORGIE: Maybe not just yet.

LEE: It's funny. Things like that happen to you, you know, you become a father, it's like you've been let into a new room. You see the whole world differently. And it's all the same people you knew before in there. But they all see things differently, all the fathers and mothers. They've been let into this secret they share, and it changes things. It changes the way that you see.

GEORGIE: That's lovely.

LEE: It's scary.

GEORGIE: Why?

LEE: You never leave the room again. You and everyone in it. Danni wants to leave me.

GEORGIE: Really?

LEE: I think so. I think she should. I'm no good for her. She hates it on the site. She isn't happy. I'm not happy either.

GEORGIE: I'm sure you are.

LEE: I'm no good for her. I'm still in love with someone else, aren't I.

GEORGIE: Lee.

LEE: Sorry.

GEORGIE: I thought you hated me. I thought you were gone. I didn't think I'd ever see you again. I didn't know you were here, did I? I didn't know how you felt. It's too late now. It's too late to say this.

LEE: Do you think we could?

GEORGIE: What?

LEE: Go off together.

GEORGIE: Of course not.

LEE: Why not?

GEORGIE: I'm married. You're married. You have a family.

LEE: Thing is I think I'm gonna lose it all anyway. I'm not good enough for them, I'm gonna lose it. Those aren't the right reasons not to run away with me by the way.

GEORGIE: What do you mean?

LEE: You said you're married, I'm married, I have a family.

GEORGIE: Yeah.

LEE: The reason you didn't run away with me should be that you don't want to.

GEORGIE: Yeah. It's not real, Lee. We're not kids, it's not a game, this is real life, it's not happening.

LEE: What would it be like if it did though, d'you think?

GEORGIE: I think I ought to go back in.

LEE: Don't you wanna do one pure thing? And push away all of the bollocks and compromises and do just one thing that you actually mean, you actually want to happen?

GEORGIE: I did it today, Lee. I got married.

LEE: My car's parked round the corner.

GEORGIE: Did you drive here?

LEE: Yeah.

GEORGIE: You're not driving it back.

LEE: Why not?

GEORGIE: How many have you had?

LEE: Only half a mile on a quiet road. But I could drive somewhere else tonight. If we wanted, we could drive anywhere. It's only this way people have of sleepwalking through everything that's stopping us, isn't it. We could go anywhere if we just woke up. Hit the road and go look for our real lives. These aren't our real lives, are they? There must be more than this. I'm gonna go and wait in my car.

GEORGIE: Don't.

LEE: No, I'll just sit in my car for a bit, I think. See whether there's anyone else here tonight who wants to be awake like I do. Maybe see you later, G.

GEORGIE: You won't.

LEE: I'll go wait anyway.

LEE exits. GEORGIE puts her head in her hands. ROB enters. He walks up behind her and puts his arms around her.

GEORGIE: Fuck off!

ROB: Hey.

GEORGIE: Oh my God it's you.

ROB: Yeah..

GEORGIE: Sorry. I didn't. I didn't hear you.

ROB: It's OK. Are you all right?

GEORGIE: No. I don't know. I'm fine, I'm fine.

ROB: Yeah?

GEORGIE: Just tired. Just tired out from dancing.

ROB: Your mum's had a lot to drink.

GEORGIE: Yeah?

ROB: She's being OK though.

GEORGIE: So far.

ROB: Yeah.

GEORGIE: You shouldn't have invited so many randomers to the evening.

ROB: Only a couple of mates.

GEORGIE: There's like eight people in there weren't on the guest list. Why did you invite Danni and Lee?

ROB: I dunno. I thought you'd like it. Don't you like it?

GEORGIE: We didn't budget for it. We won't have enough food and drink.

ROB: It'll be all right. Don't worry about it. This time tomorrow we'll be in Benahavis.

GEORGIE: Yeah.

ROB: And then we'll start. Then we'll really have started.

GEORGIE: Do you think we did all right?

ROB: Course I do.

GEORGIE: Yeah.

ROB: Tell you what Trev was fucking funny wasn't he? That's the thing about having him for a best man. Cos he literally is, like, the best man.

GEORGIE: Yeah.

ROB: What was that joke? That honeymoon joke?

GEORGIE: He said, Georgie told me they're going to Spain for honeymoon, which was confusing, cos when I asked Rob what they were doing he said he was going to Bangor for two weeks.

ROB: Fucking brilliant! Bangor! Wales! Absolute gold.

GEORGIE: Maybe.

ROB: Did you hear about my walk on music?

GEORGIE: Yeah what the hell was that?

ROB: *(Sings.)* 'It's the – eye of the tiger in the dah dah dah dah, rising up to the dah dah dah dah dah dah!'

GEORGIE: Groom's aren't even supposed to have music.

ROB: I thought it was cool.

GEORGIE: You're an idiot.

ROB: But that's why you love me.

GEORGIE: No, it's not. *(She looks at the photo of Cath.)* Do you think we'll be like that one day?

ROB: Like what?

GEORGIE: Like her and Brian.

ROB: What, dead?

GEORGIE: No, not dead. I mean old and in love with each other. He still really loves her, doesn't he. Do you think we'll be like that?

ROB: You won't love me.

GEORGIE: Why not?

ROB: When I'm old I'll fart and snore and never close the fridge.

GEORGIE: Yeah, maybe.

ROB: You all right?

GEORGIE: Tell me why you love me.

ROB: What?

GEORGIE: Tell me what it is, I don't know, I can't remember what's good about me.

ROB: Georgie.

GEORGIE: Tell me.

ROB: Well I've loved you for years. All my life nearly. Cos you were there when I started school and you seemed – on fire. You were amazing. I couldn't not look at you.

GEORGIE: Yeah?

ROB: You were so beautiful. Always so beautiful. But we never talked. And then we meet again four years later, and you're interested in me. The most beautiful girl I ever saw. I don't even know how that's happened.

GEORGIE: Is it enough d'you think?

ROB: What?

GEORGIE: Is it enough to last a lifetime? That you thought I was beautiful when we were young?

ROB: It's more than that.

GEORGIE: I'm frightened, Rob. I'm frightened I'm not good enough for you.

ROB: Don't say that. You're perfect. You're all I want, I promise. When you know, you know, right? You know it's that person you wanna be with.

GEORGIE: Yeah. Yeah, you do. Look, I just need to go to the bathroom.

ROB: OK.

GEORGIE: Then we'll have a proper boogie.

ROB: All right.

GEORGIE: Just a minute. You're lovely, Rob. I hope you know I think that.

ROB: I do.

GEORGIE: Never forget that. All right.

ROB: I'll see you inside.

GEORGIE: Yeah. Give me a minute.

GEORGIE exits. ROB looks at the remnants of the rubbish on the floor. Enter HELEN.

HELEN: She all right?

ROB: I dunno.

HELEN: But you're talking, the two of you.

ROB: Yeah. I think she's just emotional. I think she's fine.

HELEN: OK.

ROB: She's just gone to the loo. Weren't listening in on us were you?

HELEN: No.

ROB: What's wrong?

HELEN: What?

ROB: There's obviously something wrong Mum, so say it.

HELEN: There's nothing.

ROB: No, but there is. Come on.

HELEN: She hasn't got the bloom on her.

ROB: What does that mean?

HELEN: It's hard to say. But if she was happy I think – don't you think there's something missing?

ROB: No, I don't.

HELEN: I've been talking to her friend from school. Danni, the girl you invited.

ROB: Right.

HELEN: Did you know Georgie used to go out with that boy who's here tonight?

ROB: Who, Lee?

HELEN: Did she tell you that?

ROB: That's not true.

HELEN: Danni just told me.

ROB: Lee?

HELEN: Danni said he proposed to her.

ROB: What?

HELEN: Yeah. And her parents stopped it because they didn't like him. Said they were really into each other at one time. Don't you think she should have told you that?

ROB: She told me there'd been someone like that. I didn't know it was him.

HELEN: I spose if you did you probably wouldn't have invited him tonight.

ROB: No, I obviously wouldn't. She did say, I remember, she said she wanted to get married one other time. But it didn't happen. I never really asked, I thought I shouldn't.

HELEN: I have tried to raise this, Rob.

ROB: What?

HELEN: I have tried to tell you you don't know her well enough.

ROB: No, you'll have it wrong, Mum.

HELEN: You need to talk to her. You have to ask her now before it all starts snowballing, because it's hard to get out of your life once you're in it, my love. You have to choose what you throw yourself into.

Enter DANNI.

DANNI: I'm sorry.

HELEN: Oh.

DANNI: I'm sorry to bother you. Have you seen Lee? I haven't seen him. He hasn't come back in.

ROB: What?

DANNI: He went for a fag and he hasn't come back. I can't find him.

ROB: Dunno, sorry.

HELEN: Where's Georgie?

DANNI: I don't know.

HELEN: You just said she's in the loos.

ROB: Yeah.

HELEN: She not come back out yet?

DANNI: I haven't seen her in there, I've just been all round, I didn't see her.

ROB: Really?

DANNI: She'll still be in the loo. Bastards to get off, those dresses.

ROB: Yeah, sure.

HELEN: Why don't you go and check Rob?

ROB: What, go in the ladies'?

HELEN: Why don't you go and check?

ROB: OK. Fine.

HELEN: See where she's got to.

ROB exits.

HELEN: He didn't know. What you told me, she hadn't told him.

DANNI: Oh.

HELEN: He didn't know.

DANNI: She probably just felt awkward bringing it up. It'll be all right. She probably felt awkward.

HELEN: They couldn't have.

DANNI: What?

HELEN: No. Nothing.

DANNI: What?

HELEN: I was just thinking they couldn't have –

DANNI: No. No, they wouldn't do that. They wouldn't.

Enter ROB.

ROB: She's not in there.

HELEN: No?

ROB: I didn't look in the cubicles or nothing, don't worry. But she's not there.

HELEN: Right.

ROB: Bit weird.

HELEN: Yeah.

ROB: Missing half your own bloody wedding, right?

HELEN: Right.

DANNI: His car's not there.

HELEN: What?

ROB: Whose car?

HELEN: Lee's?

DANNI: We parked just there, it's gone look.

ROB: Oh.

DANNI: He shouldn't be driving. He must have gone home. He's had too much to drink. They haven't, have they?

ROB: Haven't what?

HELEN: No, no.

ROB: Haven't what?

DANNI: Gone off.

ROB: What?

HELEN: Only –

ROB: Fuck off. That's mental!

DANNI: But the car's gone.

ROB: He's gone home. Sore head.

DANNI: Why's he left me then?

ROB: No, that's mental.

HELEN: Maybe we should check the loos again for Georgie.

ROB: No Mum, I said she's not in there.

HELEN: Maybe she's by the buffet.

ROB: Oh my God they fucking have, haven't they.

DANNI: Let's go and check the buffet again, maybe.

ROB: You know she's not. When she went back in she said to me – when she left –

DANNI: They wouldn't.

ROB: Oh my God, they fucking have. Give me your keys.

HELEN: No, darling, that's not -

ROB: Give me the fucking –

ROB grabs HELEN's handbag, empties it, grabs the keys.

ROB: Why can't you just fucking do what I ask you?

HELEN: Rob. Rob!

ROB exits.

4

BRIAN enters the space. It seems we are somewhere else now, not round the back of the hall. Music under what he says, music swelling and estranging us.

BRIAN: Smile at us, pay us, pass us, but do not quite forget,
for we are the people of England, that never have spoken
yet. You didn't think I knew you were listening. Most of
the time people don't listen to folk like us, do they. The
thousands and millions glossed over every day, because
we're not all right, not really. Because these are our lives,
and we thought they might be anything, but now they're
underway it's turned out there's not all that much to them.
Not like we hoped for, like we dreamed. And it doesn't do
to think of us, and the world doesn't speak of us, because
we'd all rather pretend life's not like that, life's not made
up of almosts. Nearlies. Might have beens. Never weres.
But when you stop and think of it. Well when you stop
and think.

How can that be that our lives aren't worth hearing? How
do you know but every bird that cuts the airy way is an
immense world of delight, closed by your senses five?

Perhaps we see figures in the dark around Brian, arriving and leaving, shadows and glimpses of bodies passing by.

Every day of my life I walk these roads, these fields, in and
out of the shadow of these bungalows, and I know no one
thinks I live somewhere important. But what if that was
wrong? What if there was more to it under the surface?
What if I told you it was here twelve hundred years ago
King Alfred won the battle that first united England? It
was from behind the walls of the priory at the bottom
of this village that Guthrun sent out the terms of his
surrender, and allowed our country to come into being.
And what if I told you that five hundred years after that,

the villagers of this parish dragged the bishop of Salisbury
from out of the pulpit as he preached a sermon in the
same priory, and dragged him to the top of the hill where
the white horse is carved in chalk, and stripped him naked
and beat him to death, because they hated his protector
the king? And how many of you remember Imber, the
village that was emptied by the war, my parents relocated
to this place and never let home, exiled from their
birthright for the sake of their country? Have you dipped
your hands in the wounds of that village, stuck a finger
in the bullet holes of the ghost hovels, and understood as
I was made to understand too soon, that you know your
home for the first time once you can no longer get back
to it? Do we seem so ordinary, so small in our bungalows,
once you know all that happened here as well? Or are our
lives myths, are they poems singing under this quotidian
skin? You didn't think I knew you were listening. But
there's more to me than meets the eye. There's more to
anyone.

Cloudscapes haunt the stage.

Look at the clouds above our head. We thought we
were like them once, when we were young and easy. We
thought we could turn into anything. That could be a
whale, a ship, a dog chasing rabbits. Or it could be two
cars driven madly through the Wiltshire night. And that
there, is that a river in spate? Or is it a blind bend in the
pitchdark, a rope to strangle the panicking drivers? And is
that two lovers in the hay? Or can you see cars leaving the
ground and rolling, rolling, smashed and mangled on the
same black bend where no one can hear them in the dark
of the Wiltshire night?

The stage cracks and breaks, the set splits open, light flooding through.

This is a hungry county. In the end it claims us all and drowns us. Long time gone there was a girl from this village who drowned in a pool in the middle of the Plain. And now she lies there, so cold, because there's no lifeblood left to warm the limbs of her, and she longs for the life in all of us to keep her warm, the poor lost soul. One by one she draws us in. All my life I have watched them passing through here on their way to the girl in the bottom of the pond. She's why we're known as the moonraker county. Her bloodless face it lies in the water so pale, for all the world if you saw her where she lies and lived to tell of it, you'd swear you had been looking at the moon. Here they are, coming this way look. Here they come passing through on their way to her. Some nights you can't quite see them passing, but it's easy enough if you know where to look and the moon is full.

Enter LEE and ROB. The stage falls silent.

BRIAN: There you are, boys. There you are.

ROB: That could be a whale, a ship, a dog chasing rabbits. Or it could be two cars driven madly through the Wiltshire night.

LEE: Is that two lovers in the hay? Or can you see cars leaving the ground and rolling, rolling, smashed and mangled on the same black bend where no one can hear them in the dark of the Wiltshire night?

BRIAN: I know.

LEE: The earth and the osiers rising to drown us.

ROB: Oil on the road.

LEE: Into the river. Rolling, tearing.

ROB: Where are we?

BRIAN: Look around you. What can you see?

ROB: Only the night.

BRIAN: There you go.

LEE: So where are we?

BRIAN: You've come home to the centre, boys, home to
the Plain. This is where we end up when our myths
are finished. (*BRIAN turns back to the audience.*) Two boys
driving. Both drunk. On the right angle bend at the foot
of the Priory, where the village ends and the road speeds
up into the neverending distance, one takes things too fast
and skids, and his car flips, and he and the girl beside him
are spun like food in a blender. As if they'd reached the
end of a chain, and the chain had caught them. The girl
in the passenger seat's still conscious. She can't wake the
boy beside her. They're only children really, though they
think they know so much. She crawls out of the car to try
and drag him through the driver's door. Wedding dress
covered in his blood, not her own blood. And another
car comes screaming out of the night, faster than the first
one, too fast for the wishbone bend. He ploughs into the
first car where it lies with its wheels in the air. The girl
is standing on the verge, watching it happen. Sees the
fire start. The explosion. Who can tell the exact moment
when they died? When the flames roar over them both,
she can't bear it. She turns and runs away from what's
happened, wedding dress torn and bloodied, wedding
vows trailing behind her. She runs away, and it's twelve
hours before anyone finds her. Before she walks into the
police station, thinking she has to hand herself in. By
then both the bodies are on their slabs, and it's all over.
The fire's out, except in the eyes of everyone who saw it,
where it will never stop burning.

5

The stage clears, and day breaks, and it is the morning, exactly one year later. We watch it for a moment. We hear the sound of a car pulling up. HELEN and DANNI enter. DANNI is no longer pregnant. They are smartly and soberly dressed, and carrying bouquets of flowers.

HELEN: Here we go then.

They walk to the spot where they can see down the hill, and stand in silence for a moment.

HELEN: This was it.

DANNI: Yeah.

HELEN: Feels like you could just step back into it.

Silence.

HELEN: When he was a boy. Well he was still a boy, wasn't he. But when he was younger I used to tell him he never thought enough about things. And because of that he kept on ending up in trouble. Whenever a thought came in his head he'd just do it, and then he'd come to me with money trouble, because he'd bought something he couldn't afford, or he'd have got into trouble at school or whatever. I used to ask him, why can you never stop and think? But he'd just do whatever occurred to him.

DANNI: Do you want to go down yet?

HELEN: Just another minute yet.

Silence.

HELEN: It feels like they're still gonna be there.

DANNI: I know.

HELEN: You feel the same?

DANNI: Yeah.

HELEN: Or we think we feel the same. But who knows.

The door to the hall opens, and BRIAN enters. He is smartly and soberly dressed as well. HELEN and DANNI turn to look at him. No one speaks for a moment.

BRIAN: I wondered whether I'd see you today.

DANNI: Brian.

BRIAN: You two all right?

DANNI: All right, yeah. We just used the car park, I hope you don't mind.

BRIAN: You do whatever you want, all right? Helen?

HELEN: Hi, Brian. You've dressed up for us.

BRIAN: I thought I should, just in case.

HELEN: Well.

BRIAN: Thought of you both this morning.

DANNI: Thank you.

BRIAN: Do you want anything, either of you? I could make a cup of tea or I could walk down with you. Whatever you want.

HELEN: I think we're all right, thank you.

BRIAN: I thought you would be. Just wanted to offer.

HELEN: Thank you. You know what it's like.

BRIAN: Yeah. And I'm so sorry for you both.

HELEN: Thank you.

DANNI: Thank you.

Silence.

BRIAN: Least it's turned out clear.

DANNI: Yeah.

Silence.

HELEN: We were just talking about them.

BRIAN: Oh yeah?

HELEN: Stupid boys. Stupid, stupid boys.

BRIAN: Yeah. Have you been all right, Dan?

DANNI: Oh, yeah. I'm all right, yeah. Got my own place now.

BRIAN: Oh right?

DANNI: Cos Helen put me and the babies up at first.

BRIAN: I heard, yeah. That was very generous of you.

HELEN: It was nothing.

DANNI: Now you've got me a job at the ASDA you work at, haven't you, so now I've got that coming in on top of what I get for Kenzie and the baby, I can pay rent again.

BRIAN: Great.

DANNI: So we're in a place in Trowbridge, yeah.

BRIAN: That's great.

DANNI: A start.

BRIAN: Yeah. You done so much for her Helen, getting her a job as well.

HELEN: Least I could do.

DANNI: So we're all right, really. Finding ways. And you and me still see each other at work.

HELEN: Yeah.

DANNI: And there isn't time with the kids to think too much in the evenings.

BRIAN: I'm sure.

DANNI: So it's all right.

BRIAN: Yeah.

HELEN: Good to keep busy.

BRIAN: Isn't it, yeah.

DANNI: Thank you for asking, Brian.

BRIAN: Well maybe I should leave you to it. You'll be wanting to walk down to – to where it happened, I suppose.

DANNI: Do you ever go back? To the place where your daughter –

BRIAN: Not any more, no. I went the first year.

HELEN: I think I'll be the same.

BRIAN: Yeah?

HELEN: I was just thinking that. They're not there, are they? They're not in the place where they died. It's forgotten them. I can see the view and remember, but it's easier to visit the grave.

BRIAN: I think so, yeah. I think that's where you feel closest. Well I'll leave you both to it.

HELEN: Thank you, Brian. Very much.

BRIAN: All right. Look after each other.

The sound of a car arriving.

DANNI: Oh my God.

BRIAN: Oh, no.

DANNI: I can't fucking believe this.

Enter GEORGIE, dressed down, hood up. She takes down her hood.

BRIAN: Georgie.

GEORGIE: I'm so sorry. I didn't know you'd be here. I wanted to – I didn't think you'd come here today. I thought you'd go to the graves.

DANNI: I can't believe you'd come here today.

GEORGIE: I'm sorry, Dan.

DANNI: I can't fucking believe I've gotta see your face on top of everything else.

GEORGIE: I'm really sorry.

HELEN: All right, Danielle.

DANNI: What?

HELEN: Just breathe. All right.

GEORGIE cries.

GEORGIE: I wasn't gonna come. I didn't think I deserved to. But then last night I didn't go to bed, I couldn't shut my eyes, I was hurting. And I couldn't breathe sitting in my room like that, not doing anything. So I thought if I drove here, and came in the morning, I wouldn't see anyone, and I could just say sorry and get back in my car and maybe that would help with the feeling. I didn't know you'd be here, I'm sorry.

HELEN: Danni has the kids again from three. Life carries on, Georgina, you have to fit these kinds of things around it.

GEORGIE: Yeah. I wanted to write to you both so many times. I've thought about you both, you know. But I didn't think you'd want to hear from me.

HELEN: Yeah.

GEORGIE: I haven't gone and forgotten. Ever since the inquests, I haven't thought about anything else.

HELEN: Well.

DANNI: You gave him up. You gave him up and he was mine. Why couldn't you let me keep him?

GEORGIE: I didn't mean to do what I did. I got so lost. I didn't know what was going to happen.

DANNI: You were always like that. Never thought things through. You were always like this. What did you think you were doing?

GEORGIE: I don't know. I felt like I couldn't help myself. I was just in a river getting dragged along, like I had to. I was gonna have a life. I believed that. And then when I had to leave school, it all went wrong. I couldn't keep the shape of things in my head, I couldn't tell what I was supposed to do. And I thought getting married, I'd get it back. But then I just felt further away from who I used to be, and he was there, he was telling me I'd got it all wrong, I'd done the wrong thing. I didn't know what I was supposed to have done. I thought I was finding a way back to the middle of things.

DANNI: Fuck you, Georgie.

HELEN: All right love. She knows what she's done.

GEORGIE: Helen –

HELEN: No.

GEORGIE: What?

HELEN: That's enough now.

GEORGIE: I'm sorry.

HELEN: You've said it. It's said now. There's nothing else I
don't think.

GEORGIE: OK.

HELEN: I'm sorry, Georgie, I've nothing else for you. It's too
late now. So strange, I feel like we never did speak, not
really. I used to feel I had to hold my tongue. I shouldn't
have done. But I was scared I'd drive away my boy, he
always got angry when he couldn't have what he wanted,
when I doubted him or told him no he'd get so wild, so
I didn't say anything, though I wondered about you. I
could see plain as anyone it was happening too fast, and
I thought what's in it for her? Why's this what she wants?
A boy like him you have to understand it, but you were
already a woman. I didn't know why you wanted to go so
fast through life. Most of the time it's only the very young
can bear to go that fast, because they don't yet know what
it'll cost 'em. Now I see it. You were running. But I didn't
ask you then because I was scared I'd lose my son. There
now, isn't that a sad thing to say on today of all days? It
isn't always the loving thing to let someone alone, and
not to challenge. Sometimes it might even be right to hurt
someone, if you want them to be happy. We're cowards
when we talk ourselves out of that.

GEORGIE: I should go.

HELEN: Please don't go to the graves. I know we can't stop
you, but not today please. Not today.

GEORGIE: All right.

BRIAN: Why don't you take a walk up the hill before you go, Georgie?

GEORGIE: Sorry?

BRIAN: Just take ten minutes. There's a good view looking out over the white horse into the south. Why don't you go for a walk and let these two alone with the village? There's a bench up there that feels like it's perched at the edge of the world.

GEORGIE: All right.

BRIAN: Doesn't do to drive crying.

GEORGIE: No. All right then. Well I'll go up then. Bye.

GEORGIE exits. Silence.

DANNI: Why couldn't she just get out of here?

BRIAN: Don't be angry now. Put her out your mind. She'll be looking the other way when you lay your flowers down.

DANNI: She didn't have to come.

BRIAN: I know. But she came, so.

DANNI: Whatever.

HELEN: I didn't do anything.

BRIAN: Helen?

HELEN: I let it all happen. I didn't know it was going. Now it's gone. And I never did anything about it, never seized it, never held on. Well. You OK?

DANNI: No.

HELEN: No. No I'm not either. But I don't think there's much we can do about that.

DANNI: No. We'll have to live, I think.

HELEN: Are you ready to go down?

DANNI: Yeah.

HELEN: All right then. Let's go down.

They exit. BRIAN watches them go.